Instant Christmas Pageant:
The Fumbly Bumbly Angels

by

Sandy Cope and Sandy Dillbeck

INSTANT CHRISTMAS PAGEANT:
THE FUMBLY BUMBLY ANGELS

Copyright © 1997, 2016 Group Publishing, Inc.

Visit our website: **group.com**

All rights reserved. No part of this book may be reproduced in any manner whatsoever without prior written permission from the publisher, except where noted in the text and in the case of brief quotations embodied in critical articles and reviews. For information, visit group.com/permissions.

Credits

Authors: Sandy Cope and Sandy Dillbeck
Editor: Jody Brolsma
Chief Creative Officer: Joani Schultz
Assistant Editor: Helen Turnbull
Art Director: Jean Bruns
Cover Art Director: RoseAnne Sather
Print Production Artist: Ray Tollison
Cover Illustrator: Paula Becker
Illustrator: Megan Jeffery

Library of Congress Cataloging-in-Publication Data
Cope, Sandy.
    Instant Christmas pageant : the fumbly bumbly angels / by Sandy Cope and Sandy Dillbeck.
    p. cm.
    ISBN 978-1-4707-4279-9
    1. Christmas plays, American. 2. Angels--Drama. I. Dillbeck, Sandy. II. Title.
PS3553.063353I57 1996
    ISBN 978-1-4707-4279-9   812' .54--dc21

Printed in the United States of America.

5 4 3 2 1   20 19 18 17 16

Instant Christmas Pageant: THE FUMBLY BUMBLY ANGELS

Contents

How to Use This Pageant 4

Assigning the Roles 7

Creating the Costumes 8

Preparing the Props 12

Publicizing the Pageant 22

Setting the Stage 23

The Fumbly Bumbly Angels: The Script 25

Christmas Song Lyrics 56

HOW TO USE THIS
Pageant

Congratulations! Most of the hard work in preparing your children's Christmas pageant is already done! You hold the result of that work in your hands right now—*The Fumbly Bumbly Angels,* an Instant Christmas Pageant.

The Fumbly Bumbly Angels provides you with a complete Christmas program on compact disc. All the spoken dialogue, sound effects, and music are prerecorded. You even get songs for the whole congregation to sing along with the children.

This Instant Christmas Pageant is flexible. Your kids can perform it for:
- a Sunday morning service,
- an afternoon or evening children's program,
- a family night program,
- a special Sunday school program,
- a nursing home program, and more!

And it can be performed by children from ages four through eighty-four.

Even teenagers and senior citizens will enjoy putting on this pageant! Or you can have a puppet group perform the pageant.

The Fumbly Bumbly Angels is easy to prepare for, too. Just follow these simple steps:

1. Read the rest of this book, and listen to the CD.

2. Photocopy the clip art on page 22 to decorate fliers, bulletins, and posters publicizing the pageant. You'll also find clip art on *The Fumbly Bumbly Angels* CD. Simply put the CD into any Macintosh- or IBM-compatible CD-ROM drive, and read the instructions in the "Read Me" file to use clip art that'll create dynamite publicity pages!

3. Determine how you'll adjust the number of roles in the play to match the number of children who'll be in your program. You'll find a few ideas on page 7 on how to add or subtract to the roles.

4. Have kids help you collect and create costumes and props. Many props can be collected from kids' homes. And you can create the rest using the photocopiable patterns beginning on page 13.

5. Play the CD for your children. Then assign parts to children.

6. Practice the play with your children. Here's the fun part—kids don't need to memorize their lines! Don't have them lip-sync the parts, either. Instead, direct kids to follow the action and movement instructions in the script. After one or two times through, kids will know how to pantomime all the actions needed! Or have kids come up with their own actions.

7. Perform the play. During the play, invite the congregation to sing along with the Christmas carols.

It's that simple!

Here are a few tips to help you get the most of *The Fumbly Bumbly Angels:*

- Practice the actions and movements a few times so kids feel comfortable with their roles before a performance.

❶ - Refer to the CD icon (see margin) throughout the script to find exactly where the CD selections occur in the pageant. That way you'll be able to practice a particular segment of the script without hunting for the corresponding CD selection.

- Because each setup is different, you may want to pause the CD during the pageant, allowing time for kids to move across the stage.

- Have a child or adult volunteer introduce the pageant before hitting the "play" button on your CD player. This is a good time to let the congregation know they'll be singing along during the pageant.

- Use teenagers, adults, or senior citizens to supplement roles if you don't have a large enough group of children.

- Increase the length of your program by having children read aloud sections of Luke's account of Jesus' birth before, during, or after the play.

- Read and discuss Luke 2:1-20 with your children as you prepare for the program. Use the costume-creation times and rehearsal times as mini-Bible studies.

> *Helpful Hint*
> You might want to have the Fumbly, Bumbly Angels and the Archangel practice separately a few times since it might take more time to learn movements to the words.

Assigning the *Roles*

One of the best features of *The Fumbly Bumbly Angels* is that any child in your church can play almost any role. Since the spoken parts are prerecorded and kids don't need to memorize lines, younger children can become the main characters as easily as older children. The role of the Archangel is probably best suited to an older child or an adult since an older and wiser appearance is essential for the part.

Each role in *The Fumbly Bumbly Angels* is listed in the "Creating the Costumes" section (p. 8).

If you have fewer than twenty-two children, have only one Sheep, three Travelers, and one Shepherd. Or have the same children who play the Travelers also be the Innkeeper and/or the Shepherds and/or the Three Kings. Or teenagers and adults can help out by playing such roles as the Three Kings, Mary and Joseph, the Shepherd, the Innkeeper, and the Archangel.

If you have more than twenty-two children, increase the number of Travelers, Sheep, Shepherds, and young Angels for the Heavenly Choir during the finale. Or form a separate children's choir to lead the congregation in singing the hymns.

CREATING THE
Costumes

Costume elements and props are suggested in this section for each character. Using the prop instructions and patterns beginning on page 13, you can create costume elements such as halos, kings' crowns, sheep ears, the star of Bethlehem, and sheet music.

ARCHANGEL — *The Angel in charge who is older and regal in appearance. The Archangel gives the Fumbly, Bumbly Angels their instructions. His attire is noticeably more pristine than the younger Angels.*

Suggested costume attire: White sweat pants or slacks, a white long-sleeve shirt, and a pair of white socks work best. Sandals are worn for shoes. Drape a white sheet around the shoulders. (See page 13 for details.) For an added "heavenly" effect, outline the sheet in gold garland or glitter glue. Create a halo with gold garland using the pattern on page 13.

CHANCE — *A Fumbly, Bumbly Angel. This Angel is clumsy, with a happy "cool dude" attitude. Most likely a boy.*

Suggested costume attire: White pants, shirt, socks, and sandals. Drape a sheet over his shoulders. (See page 13 for details.) A brightly colored handkerchief hangs loosely from waistband. He needs to have a pocket or someplace to tuck an envelope. Fill Chance's pockets with miscellaneous "junk" items such as gum wrappers, marbles, a plastic frog, and a slingshot. Create a halo with silver garland using the pattern on page 13.

DAPHNE— *A Fumbly, Bumbly Angel. This Angel has a lighthearted and "dipsy" personality. Most likely a girl.*

Suggested costume attire: Same as other Fumbly, Bumbly Angels. Her halo always sits haphazardly on her head.

PENELOPE— *A Fumbly, Bumbly Angel. This persnickety Angel is always prim and proper. Most likely a girl.*

Suggested costume attire: Same as other Fumbly, Bumbly Angels. Her attire is neat and her hair is precisely styled.

GEORGE— *A Fumbly, Bumbly Angel. This well-groomed Angel has a serious, mature attitude. Most likely a boy.*

Suggested costume attire: Same as other Fumbly, Bumbly Angels. His halo is large and (to his dismay) is constantly falling down around his shoulders.

TRAVELERS— *People from all around the country coming to Bethlehem to be counted for the census. They are dressed in assorted attire.*

Suggested costume attire: Bathrobes or any garment that hangs long. These can be draped with a shawl or another piece of material. These items should be worn over the children's own clothing. Some Travelers can wear headdresses (towels draped over their heads with ties to secure them). Sandals can be worn for shoes.

Give each Traveler a bundle or cloth bag to carry.

SHEPHERDS— *Two shepherds sent by an Angel to the manger to see Jesus.*

Suggested costume attire: Headdresses (a towel placed over the head with a tie to secure it) and bathrobes. Shepherds can wear sandals. Give each Shepherd a long staff made from a wooden dowel rod, a cane, or a large stick cut from a tree.

SHEEP— *Herded by the shepherds. Dressed in white, the sheep crawl along the floor in front of the shepherds, bleating.*

Suggested costume accessories: White sweat pants, shirt, and socks. (Patterns and instructions for sheep's tail, topknot, and ears are on pages 14-15.) The number of Sheep is optional depending on the number of children you have to work with. If there aren't enough kids to be Sheep, the Shepherds can pretend to be herding sheep with their staffs.

INNKEEPER— *The keeper of the inn. This grumpy man or woman scowls a lot and is obviously unfriendly.*

Suggested costume attire: Bathrobe, headdress, and sandals.

THREE KINGS— *People of high rank who bring gifts to baby Jesus. The Kings walk proud and tall, carrying themselves with dignity.*

Suggested costume attire: Brightly colored bathrobes and sandals. (Use patterns on page 16 to make kings' crowns.) Add ornate necklaces, rings, or bracelets. Each King carries a gift wrapped in shiny paper or cloth.

MARY AND JOSEPH— *The earthly parents of baby Jesus. They are pure and wholesome. They wear pleasant smiles at all times, radiating peace and serenity.*

Suggested costume attire: Bathrobes, sandals, and headdresses. You might want to drape them in colorful cloth scarves or sheets.

HEAVENLY CHOIR — *Angels that have descended from heaven to sing for the Lord. This choir joins the stage on the finale song and surrounds the manger.*

Suggested costume attire: Same as the Fumbly, Bumbly Angels. (See page 13 for details on Angel costumes.) Four of the Angels should be younger children.

PREPARING THE
Props

You'll create most of the props for *The Fumbly Bumbly Angels* from the patterns or instructions on the following pages. We've made the patterns photocopiable so you can distribute them to your adult helpers. Permission to photocopy the handouts from Instant Christmas Pageant: *The Fumbly Bumbly Angels* granted for local church use. (Copyright © Group Publishing, Inc., P.O. Box 481, Loveland, CO 80539.)

In addition to the props, you'll need these items:

- each character's suggested costume accessories
- colorful markers or poster paints
- a laundry basket containing two or three extra halos (one is unfinished), a white sheet, and white socks (one needs a hole in its toe)
- a refrigerator box
- a trouble light or bright flashlight
- two envelopes—one marked "orders" and the other marked "destination" in large letters
- bags of fiberfill or cotton balls
- duct tape or electrical tape
- camping lanterns
- a toy crib or cradle, or a crate or box with straw or shredded newspaper
- a doll to be the baby Jesus
- a ladder on which to hang the star of Bethlehem (optional)

● CD player and *The Fumbly Bumbly Angels* CD

Photocopy the prop patterns on stiff paper, and follow the instructions in the provided illustrations to create the props used in the pageant.

PROP INSTRUCTIONS AND PATTERNS

Angel Gowns

1. Fold sheet in half.
2. Mark the center, and cut a hole large enough for a head to fit through.
3. Take a white belt or tie, go under the back side and over and around the front side of the sheet, and tie it.
4. Trim the Archangel's gown with gold garland or glitter glue.

Halo

1. Bend a wire coat-hanger to form a circle. Straighten the hook, and wrap it around the halo, then use duct tape to cover the sharp end. You may need to adjust the size of each circle to fit each child's head, but be sure to make George's halo slightly bigger so it slips down.
2. Lace silver garland around the wire, then tape the end to the wire.
3. The Archangel's halo can be laced in gold to match the gown.

Sheep's Topknot

1. Make two holes on opposite sides of a paper plate.
2. Loop a white shoestring or ribbon through the holes on the underside.
3. Glue clumps of polyester fiber or cotton balls to the top of the plate.
4. Tie the strings underneath child's chin.

Sheep's Tail

Photocopy and cut out the pattern. Glue cotton balls or polyester fiber to the tail.
Use duct tape to secure the tail to the back of the child's waistband.

Sheep's Ears

Photocopy and cut out the pattern. Color the center of the ears pink, then glue cotton balls or polyester fiber to the outside of each ear. Tape the ears to the sides of the sheep's topknot, to a headband, or to barrettes.

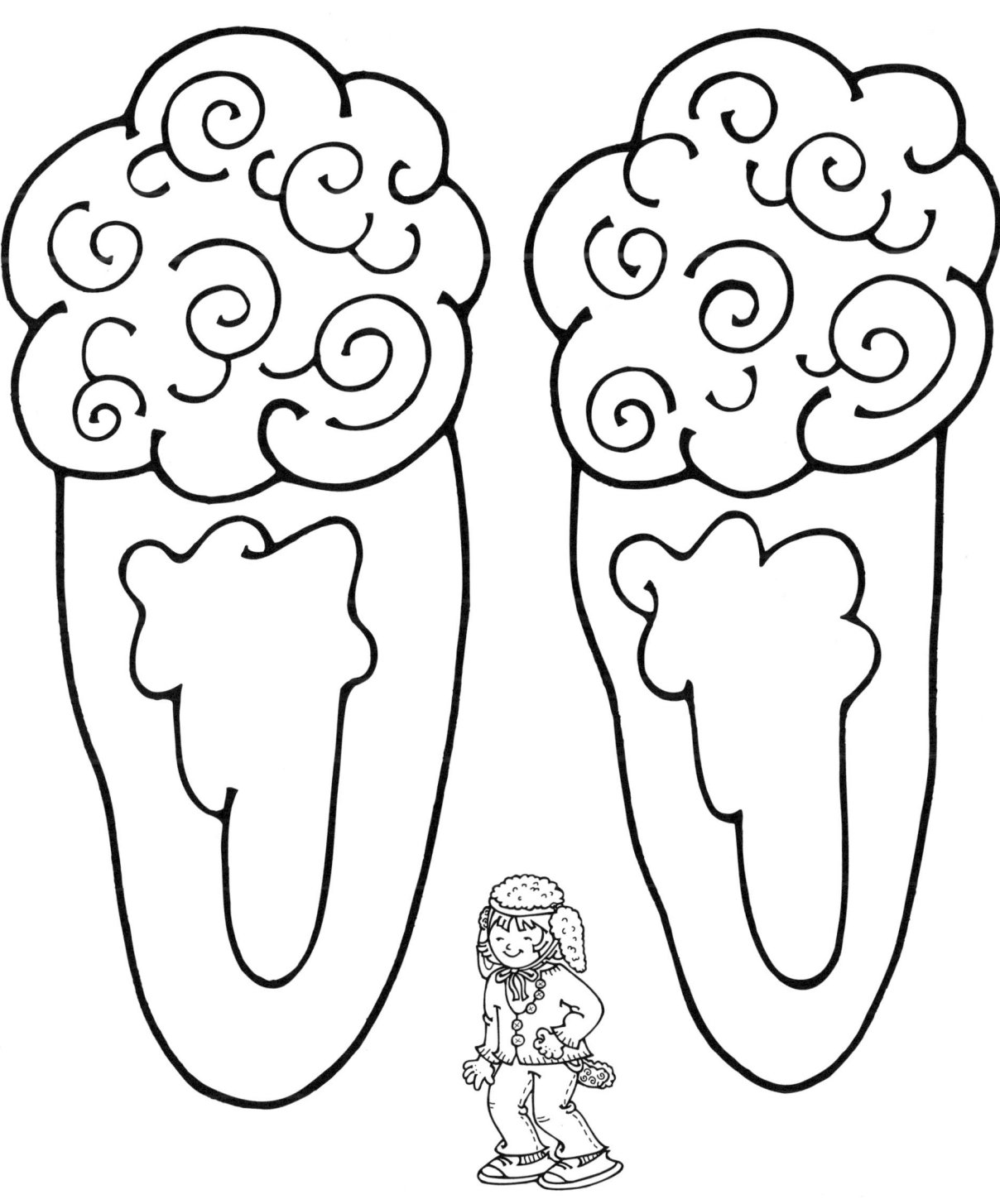

Kings' Crowns

Enlarge the patterns and cut them out. Decorate each crown with glitter glue or brightly colored markers. Tape or staple on an extra strip of paper to make the crown fit the child's head.

Star of Bethlehem

Enlarge the pattern on stiff paper or poster board, then cut out the star and cut a hole in the middle. Cover the star with foil, and place a trouble light through the center hole to shine over the manger. Hang the light from a permanent fixture in the church or use a large stepladder placed behind the manger scene.

No Vacancy Sign

Photocopy and cut out the sign. Color it with bright markers or poster paints.

Bethlehem Inn Sign

Photocopy and cut out the sign. Color it with bright markers or poster paints.

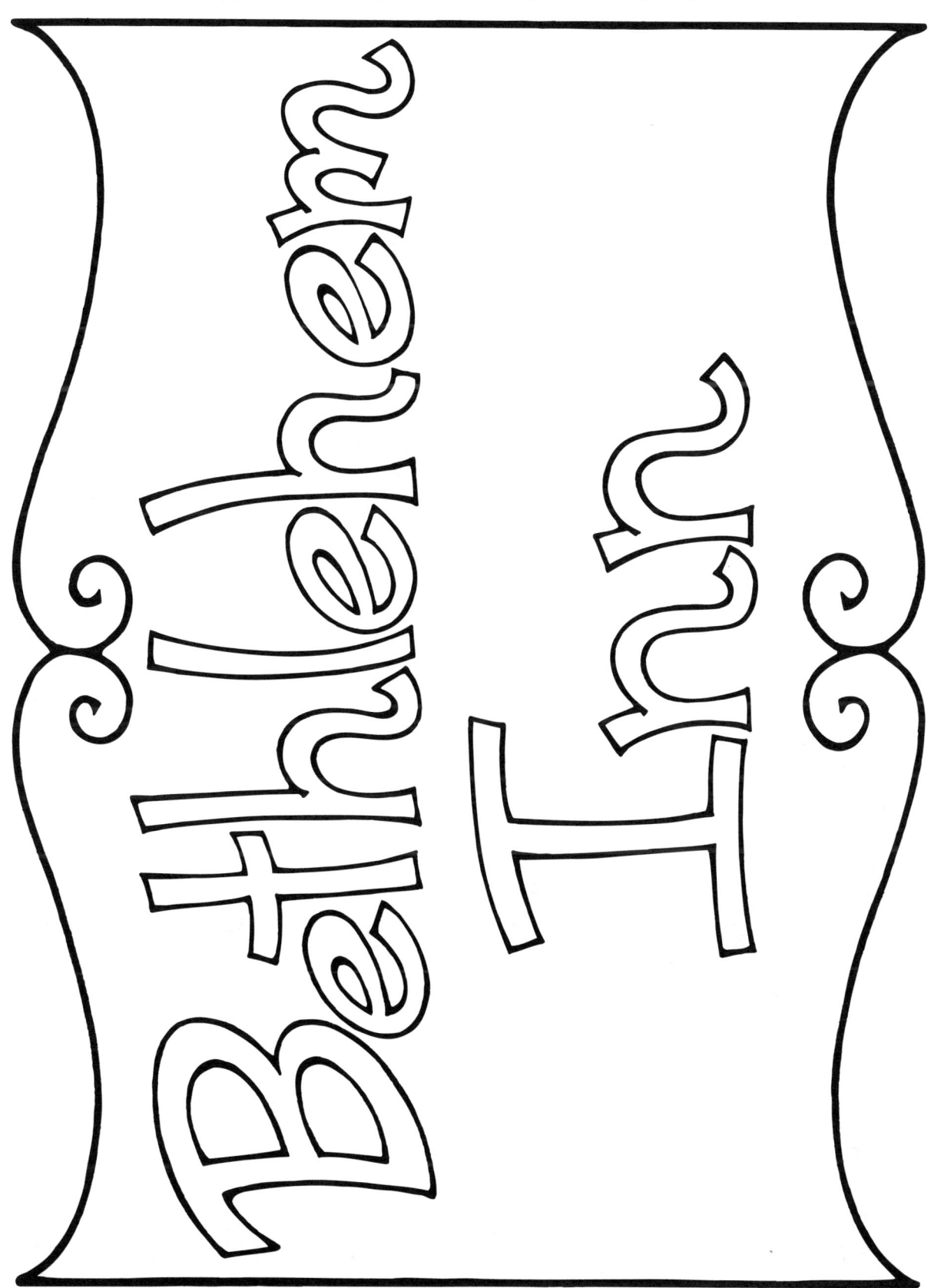

19

Destination Map

Enlarge and color the pattern. Fold up the map and place it inside the envelope marked "destination."

Sheet Music

Enlarge the pattern, and make a copy for each Fumbly, Bumbly Angel. Glue each pattern onto a white sheet of cardboard or poster board. You might want to outline each sheet with gold garland or glitter glue. Use glitter glue to add a Fumbly, Bumbly Angel's name in the box on each sheet.

PUBLICIZING THE
Pageant

Photocopy the clip art on this page to publicize your children's performance of *The Fumbly Bumbly Angels*. Use the clip art on fliers, bulletins, or posters. Or simply add the appropriate performance information to the half-page flier below to use as a bulletin insert.

Permission to photocopy this handout from *Instant Christmas Pageant: The Fumbly Bumbly Angels* granted for local church use. Copyright © Group Publishing, Inc., P.O. Box 481, Loveland, CO 80539.

Date:

Time:

Place:

Setting the *Stage*

Use the following instructions and diagram to set your stage. Adjust the location of props according to the space you have in your church.

Set up the Heaven scene at stage right. This is where the opening scene takes place. The Streets of Bethlehem scene will be performed at center stage and the Stable scene is at stage left. For the stable, simply darken that portion of the room. Light a few camping lanterns, and place them on either side of the Stable scene. Set a wooden or cardboard box on the floor, place straw or shredded paper in it, then set a doll in the "manger." Have Mary and Joseph sit near the box.

If space is restricted, after a scene has ended, move the props to either stage left or stage right to make room for the next scene. This would allow each scene to take place center stage.

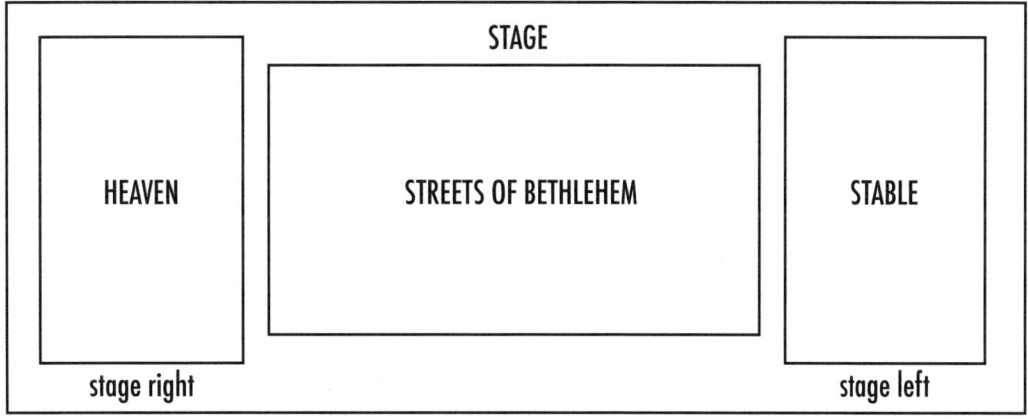

SCENE SETUPS

Heaven Scene

1. Arrange four chairs in a semicircle. (If desired, drape white or light-blue sheets over the chairs. To avoid falls, tuck loose ends of the sheets under the chairs.)

2. Use polyester fiber as fluff for clouds. Spread polyester fiber around the floor and near the chairs. Use duct tape or electrical tape to secure polyester fiber to

the floor. You can also cut cloud shapes from poster board and glue cotton balls to each cloud. Or stuff white pillowcases with newspaper to make them look like fluffy clouds. Scatter the pillowcase "clouds" around your stage area.

Bethlehem Inn Door

1. Cut a door out of one side of a large refrigerator box. Be sure you make only three cuts, so the door will open and close.

2. Use markers or paint to color the box dark brown and the door light tan.

3. Attach the "Bethlehem Inn" sign (p. 19) at the top of the box.

4. Attach the "No Vacancy" sign (p. 18) on the door.

THE FUMBLY BUMBLY ANGELS:
The Script

Use this script to familiarize yourself with the dialogue and actions in *The Fumbly Bumbly Angels*. Remember, kids don't need to memorize these lines or even lip-sync the words.

Scattered throughout the script are suggestions to assist you in planning the movement and action for the Christmas pageant. Your kids may think up new ideas and actions—that's great! Incorporate their ideas into the pageant as much as possible.

Allow someone to introduce the pageant and to remind the congregation that they'll be singing along with the carols during the program. Introduce the song "Go Tell It on the Mountain" to begin the program.

> **Helpful Hint**
> The songs in *The Fumbly Bumbly Angels* are familiar Christmas carols. But just in case some congregation members don't know all the words, photocopy the flier on page 56, and pass out copies at the beginning of the pageant.

THE PAGEANT

MARY and JOSEPH quietly enter while the congregation sings "Go Tell It on the Mountain." They take their seats near the manger. They sit motionless with their heads down throughout the play until the Stable scene near the end of the play.

❷ When the congregation stops singing, the FOUR FUMBLY, BUMBLY ANGELS enter and take their seats among the clouds in "Heaven." A laundry basket sits in front of them, overflowing with angel attire that needs to be mended. Three ANGELS take something from the basket and begin working. CHANCE takes off one sandal and inspects it.

DAPHNE begins working on the sock with the hole in it. CHANCE fumbles with his broken sandal, trying to mend it. GEORGE is wrapping a halo with garland. Much to his dismay, his own halo, which is too large, keeps falling down around his shoulders. PENELOPE is meticulously mending an angel robe (a white sheet) that rests in her lap. DAPHNE is darning socks.

The ANGELS begin their vocal practice by comically running up and down the scales, loosening their vocal chords. At the same time, DAPHNE sticks her hand in the sock, quickly discovers she has made a puppet, and uses it to lip-sync her words as she sings.

ACTIONS	WORDS
CHANCE	
	(Singing) **Do, do, do, do, do, do, do, do...**
GEORGE	
	(Singing) **Do, re, mi, fa, sol, la, ti, do...**
PENELOPE	
	(Singing) **Ah, ah, ah, ah, ah, ah, ah...**

ACTIONS	WORDS
DAPHNE	
Uses the sock with a hole in it as puppet to "sing" the scales.	*(Singing)* **Do, re, mi. Do, re, mi. Do, re, mi. Do, do, do, do, re, mi. Do, do, do, re miiiiiiiiiiiiiiii...**
The other ANGELS cringe as DAPHNE gets carried away with her singing and puppetry. They stop and frown at her antics.	
DAPHNE	
Sticks her finger out of the hole near the toe of the sock and wiggles it like a tongue with great animation.	**Aaaaaaaaaa-mmmeeeeeennnn!**
The other ANGELS roll their eyes.	
Smiles sweetly.	**How was that?**
PENELOPE	
Rubs ear with finger, as if Daphne's singing hurt her ears.	**We are simply pathetic.**
CHANCE	
Dances in his seat.	**I don't know, Penelope, I thought Daphne was kinda jammin'.**
DAPHNE	
Smiles proudly, then turns to George.	**Thank you, Chance. So what did you think, George?**

ACTIONS	WORDS
GEORGE	
	I think we're all in a jam. And it's gonna take a doozy of a miracle to get us up there...
Points upward.	...in the Heavenly Choir.
The ANGELS pause as they hear three bells chime consecutively. All the ANGELS look up as CHANCE counts aloud.	
CHANCE	
Uses fingers to count.	One...two...three...
DAPHNE	
Claps with excitement.	Oh joy! Three more angels just earned their places in the Heavenly Choir!
PENELOPE	
Suddenly pricks her finger and frowns.	Ouch! My finger!...And here we sit...
GEORGE	
Sets down the halo he's mending.	...songless...

ACTIONS	WORDS
DAPHNE	
Paces the floor frantically, getting faster as she goes.	*(Worried, Daphne begins to whine and ramble uncontrollably.)* **What if we never make it into the choir? What if they run out of room? What if we sound like a flock of screeching geese for the rest of our angelic lives? What will we do? We'll just be honks in the wind.**
Flaps arms like a goose.	*(Daphne pathetically honks and yodels like a goose.)* **Ahhonk. Ahhonk. Ahhonk.**
The other ANGELS hold their ears in agony.	
PENELOPE	
Grabs Daphne by the shoulders to stop her from pacing. DAPHNE looks bewildered. Sits down and continues her work.	**Daphne!...Dear, you're rambling again. Of course we're going to make it. We're Angels...Heaven forbid there be an angel in the clouds that doesn't sing in the choir. You're such a worrywart.**
GEORGE	
Jumps up. Fumbles with the halo he's fixing and drops it.	**You know why we're not in the choir, don't you? We've never finished an assignment. We always fumble and bumble it up.**

ACTIONS	WORDS
ALL ANGELS (Except DAPHNE)	
CHANCE knocks on his head, GEORGE waves his hand in front of Daphne's eyes, PENELOPE rolls her eyes in aggravation.	**Hello. Knock. Knock. Heaven to Daphne.**
DAPHNE	
"Wakes up" from her dazed look.	*(Innocently)* **What?**
PENELOPE	
Points to herself, then flaps arms, imitating Daphne.	**I, for one, am tired of yodeling like a honking goose. It's embarrassing.**
GEORGE	
Looks upward. Tosses another halo from the laundry basket.	**Someday we'll get our voices and be promoted upstairs, then someone else can do all this mending and repairing.**
CHANCE	
Holds up his sandal.	**I pray we get to move up the ranks soon. The tread on my sandals is wearing a little thin.**
PENELOPE	
Puts finger to temple, as if thinking.	**I was so certain we'd get our promotion after that last assignment in the desert.**

ACTIONS	WORDS

DAPHNE

Makes a face and wiggles fingers to imitate the "creepy crawly" things.	**Ooh, those awful scorpions and lizards...and those dreadful spitting camels we had to ride.**

GEORGE

Points to Daphne.	**Well, at least you *got* to ride.**

CHANCE

Holds up the foot without a sandal for the Angels to see, wiggling his toes.	**Yeah! Oh, my poor aching feet.**

ALL ANGELS (Except CHANCE)

The rest of the ANGELS frown and hold their noses in disgust.	**Pew-eee!**

CHANCE

Puts foot down and shrugs.	*(Innocently)* **What?**

❸ The ARCHANGEL enters from behind the Heaven scene carrying two envelopes tucked in his robe. He stands near the Angels on the left side of stage right. As he calls out each Angel's name, they rise and stand next to him.

ACTIONS	WORDS
ARCHANGEL	
	Okay, Angels. Roll call...Stand when I call your name...George?
GEORGE	
Stands.	Here.
ARCHANGEL	
	Penelope?
PENELOPE	
Stands.	Present.
ARCHANGEL	
	Chance?
CHANCE	
Stands.	Yo!
ARCHANGEL	
	Daphne?
DAPHNE doesn't answer and remains seated.	Daphne? Are you here?
DAPHNE	
Twisting feet nervously.	Well...I...I don't know. Do I have to ride one of those spittin' camels?

ACTIONS	WORDS

ARCHANGEL

Waves index finger in a circle.	**Nooooo. The last camel you rode is still dizzy from you talking in circles. There will be no camel rides for you today.**

DAPHNE

Quickly takes her place with the other Angels.	**Oh. Well, okay then. I guess I'm here.**

ARCHANGEL

Paces back and forth in front of Angels like a drill sergeant.	**Okay, Angels, listen up. You have a very important assignment. You've been chosen to be the bearer of good tidings at a very special event, one that will save all people on earth.**

ALL ANGELS

	Wow!

ARCHANGEL

	So the Boss has sent down two special envelopes.
Pulls out an envelope.	**One has the directions to your destination...**
Pulls out second envelope.	

ACTIONS	WORDS
Puts envelopes together.	...The other has your orders of what you should do once you get there. Put them together and what have you got?...A place in the *Heavenly Choir!* Think you can handle it?

GEORGE

Salutes.	Yes, sir!

CHANCE

Pats Archangel on the back.	No problem.

PENELOPE

Nods emphatically.	Absolutely.

DAPHNE

Claps delicately.	Oh, goody! A mystery.

ARCHANGEL

Holds out envelopes.	Who wants to be in charge of the envelopes?

CHANCE

Jumps forward, waving his arms.	I will! I will!
The rest of the ANGELS sigh and shake their heads.	

ACTIONS	WORDS
PENELOPE	
Pulls Chance back.	Oh, not you, Chance. You always lose everything.
CHANCE	
Shakes head.	I do not.
DAPHNE	
Nods head.	Yes, you dooooo.
CHANCE	
Shakes head, then looks down as if he's misplaced something.	No, I don't. Hey, anyone seen my sandal?
PENELOPE	
	Need we say more?
GEORGE	
Puts an arm around Penelope.	Ah, Penelope, let him carry the envelopes. I'll keep an eye on him.
ARCHANGEL	
Hands Chance the two envelopes.	Well, Chance, here you go. Take good care of them.
CHANCE	
Clasps envelopes to his chest.	Gee, thanks! You can count on me. We'll be singing with the other angels before you know it.

ACTIONS	WORDS
CHANCE	
Turns to the audience and says...	But until we join the Heavenly Choir, will you join us in singing, "Angels We Have Heard on High"?
❹ The ANGELS lead the audience in song.	SONG: "Angels We Have Heard on High"
ARCHANGEL	
❺ Begins pacing again like a drill sergeant when the song is finished.	Okay, Angels, you're ready to go. So strap those sandals on and hit the trail...heaven's counting on you. This is one of the biggest days in all of creation. So don't fumble-bumble it up.
ALL ANGELS	
All the ANGELS wave goodbye to the ARCHANGEL as he exits.	Goodbye!
GEORGE	
Stands near Chance and waves his hands excitedly.	This sounds like some heavy duty stuff. Hurry up, Chance. Open up the envelope. Let's see where we're going.

ACTIONS	WORDS

CHANCE

Stuffs the "orders" envelope loosely in his pocket and begins to open the "destination" envelope.	**Easy, Dude. Keep your halo on.**

DAPHNE

Clasps hands dreamily.	**Oh, I hope it's some place warm and bubbly, don't you Penelope?**

PENELOPE

Opens arms wide, to indicate the whole world.	**I don't care where it is, as long as it helps us get in the choir.**

ALL ANGELS

The ANGELS peer over Chance's shoulder.	*(Gasp with shock as they read aloud)* **Bethlehem!**

DAPHNE

Pretends to count the other Angels.	**Hey! That's where they're taking the census. You know, counting people...or is it sheep?**

CHANCE

Knocks on his head. Shakes his head.	**Hello. Knock, knock. Heaven to Daphne. It's not sheep they're counting...**

PENELOPE

Opens arms wide to indicate "multitudes."	**It's people. "Multitudes" of people.**

ACTIONS	WORDS
GEORGE	
Sticks out his elbows and pretends to be jostled around.	"Bumper-to-bumper" people.
CHANCE	
Holds foot and hops up and down.	"Steppin'-on-my-poor-achin' toes" people.
DAPHNE	
Looks at Chance's foot. Holds hands a few feet apart, as if measuring.	**Oh, my...that would hurt, wouldn't it?...All those people in that little town?**
Turns to audience.	**Please help us sing, "O Little Town of Bethlehem."**
❻	**SONG: "O Little Town of Bethlehem"**
After the song is finished, all the ANGELS look down through the clouds at the city of Bethlehem by looking down and toward center stage.	
GEORGE	
❼ Points to Bethlehem. Motions to Penelope.	**Well, there it is, and all that goes with it...** **...Ladies first, Penelope.**

ACTIONS	WORDS

PENELOPE

Shakes her head "no."	**Oh, I don't think so.**

CHANCE

Looks from Angel to Angel.	**Well, somebody's gotta jump.**

DAPHNE

Without hesitating, DAPHNE jumps over the imaginary line to center stage, flailing her arms and legs excitedly. After she "lands," she steps aside for the next Angel to follow.	**I'll go. Wheeeeeeee!**

CHANCE

Takes a giant leap and jumps.	**Geronimo!**

PENELOPE

Holds out her angel skirt, prim and proper, and tests the line with her toe, then delicately steps over the line.	**Oh...Oh, mercy me.**

GEORGE

Steps up to the line and bravely clears his throat as he stretches his arms and pops his knuckles.	**Look out below!**

❽ CENTER STAGE–Immediately the streets of Bethlehem fill with TRAVELERS scurrying about carrying satchels, backpacks, and bundles.

ACTIONS	WORDS
The ANGELS, who are bunched together, are pushed and shoved as they try to make their way from back center stage to front center stage through the crowded street.	

CHANCE

Carries one broken sandal, limps, and jumps from spot to spot as if people are stepping on his toes.	**Ouch! Ooh! Owee! Oh!**

PENELOPE

Tries to stay in the middle of the Angels in order to avoid getting her angel gown ruffled.	**Heavens to Betsy! I've never seen so many people. This is worse than the day Moses parted the Red Sea.**

GEORGE

Readjusts his large halo.	**Well, at least it's a lot drier.**

CHANCE

Hugs himself, trying to stay warm.	**Yeah, but it's a lot colder. I'm freezing my toes off.**

DAPHNE

Prances and jumps in small circles, dodging travelers.	**I don't even have a place to stand! And it's starting to get dark!**

GEORGE

Looks around, confused.	**Chance, you got our "destination" envelope. I think we better have a look at the map.**

ACTIONS	WORDS
CHANCE	
As CHANCE pulls the "destination" envelope from his pocket, the other envelope falls to the ground, unnoticed by everyone but Daphne. A TRAVELER unknowingly kicks it aside.	**Hey, you can count on me.**
PENELOPE	
Pulls Chance to one side, away from the "lost" envelope.	**Well, don't dawdle. Where do we go next?**
PENELOPE and GEORGE huddle with Chance to study the map.	
DAPHNE kneels and picks up the dropped envelope, then becomes distracted by two SHEPHERDS herding some SHEEP from back center stage slowly across to stage left. One of the shepherds is counting Sheep. DAPHNE jumps to her feet and excitedly tugs at the other Angels, trying to get their attention, but they ignore her.	
DAPHNE	
Hugs self, pretending to rub "furry" sheep wool.	**Oh, look! Sheep! I love sheep! Oh, they're so soft and furry and white. I love white. And sheep don't spit like camels do...do they?**

ACTIONS	WORDS

DAPHNE

Turns to the other Angels, pointing to the Shepherds and Sheep for the others to see, but they do not hear her.	**See? They are so counting sheep.**
Turns her attention back to the Shepherds.	**So, what brings you to Bethlehem on such a cold winter's night?**

FIRST SHEPHERD

Points up excitely.	**A sign from God.**

SECOND SHEPHERD

Excitedly opens arms wide, showing the number of angels that came.	**Angels came and told us about a baby. A very special baby.**

FIRST SHEPHERD

Turns to the audience.	**Will you help us to sing, "The First Noel"?**

❾

	SONG: "The First Noel"

DAPHNE

❿

After the song ends, the SHEPHERDS exit quickly.	
	Hey! I wanna go, too. Wait up.
Follows the Shepherds and the Sheep to the darkness of stage left...unnoticed by the other Angels who are still huddled over the map.	

42

ACTIONS	WORDS
CHANCE	
Points to a spot on the map.	**Well, "X" marks the spot.**
GEORGE	
	And "X" marks a stable.
PENELOPE	
Smacks head with hand. Holds her nose.	**A stable? You mean with hay and animals? How could a grand event, one of the greatest days in all creation, happen in a lowly, smelly stable?**
CHANCE	
Suddenly looks up and glances around.	**Hey, where's Daphne?**
GEORGE	
The other ANGELS look around.	**She was here a moment ago.**
PENELOPE	
Throws arms up in disbelief.	**Oh, for heaven's sake. I don't believe this. We've lost an angel.**
GEORGE	
	Let's find out what our orders are, and then we'll go look for Daphne. Chance, let's see the other envelope.

ACTIONS	WORDS

CHANCE

Pulls out a number of items, such as a gum wrapper, a plastic frog, a marble, and a slingshot. Frantically searches for the missing envelope as he empties his pocket. Gives the other Angels a sick look.	Uh oh.

GEORGE

Motions to Chance excitedly.	**What? What?!**

CHANCE

Puts hand to forehead.	**I think I lost it.**

PENELOPE

Walking in circles nervously.	**Oh, I knew it! I knew it! I knew it! I knew it! Not only have we lost Daphne, now we've lost the envelope.**
CHANCE gives a sheepish look.	

PENELOPE

Loses control, grabs Chance, and shakes him furiously.	**Oh! You fumbly, bumbly little Angel! We're never going to get to sing in the choir! What happened to "you can count on me"? I dare say.**

ACTIONS	WORDS
CHANCE	
Looks from Angel to Angel.	*(Sniffling)*
Pulls out a handkerchief and blows his nose loudly.	**I'm so sorry, Penelope. I'm sorry, George. I didn't mean to lose it.**
GEORGE	
George and Penelope give Chance a sour look.	**Okay. Okay. Everybody just calm down.**
CHANCE	
Immediately recovers and tosses the handkerchief over his shoulder and smiles.	**Okay.**
GEORGE	
Puts arms around other Angels.	**Nobody's going to fumble-bumble this up. We're going to stick together and see this through. We're Angels and we're gonna act like it.**
PENELOPE	
Shakes Chance's hand apologetically.	**You're right, George. I'm sorry, Chance. Sometimes I get a little carried away.**
CHANCE	
	No problem, Dudette.

ACTIONS	WORDS

GEORGE

Motions toward Bethlehem.	**All right, Angels, here's the plan. First we're going to spread out and find Daphne. Then we'll worry about the envelope and the choir later. Now let's go.**
Claps as if breaking a huddle.	

⑪ The ANGELS scurry through the thinning crowd, frantically searching for Daphne as they ask various Travelers about her.

CHANCE

Corners Traveler #1 and tries to describe Daphne to him or her by holding his hands up.	**Have you seen an angel about so tall?**

TRAVELER #1

Busily shakes his or her head "no."	**Nope. Sorry.**

TRAVELER #1 exits stage. CHANCE moves on.

GEORGE

Stops Traveler #2.	**She's dressed in white, with this cute little halo that sits cockeyed on her head.**
Jerks his halo in a cockeyed manner on his head to demonstrate.	

ACTIONS	WORDS

TRAVELER #2

Shakes his or her head "no."	**Halo? What...I don't think so.**
TRAVELER #2 exits the stage. GEORGE moves on.	

PENELOPE

Stops Traveler #3 and is trying to mimic Daphne's antics and imitating her rambling.	**She's an angel that talks like this...just rambles on and on. Chipper all the time...and prances around flailing her arms like this...She can't sit still and some times she goes "wheeeee!"**
Takes a deep breath and composes herself.	**So...have you seen her?**

TRAVELER #3

Looks at Penelope as if she's crazy and frantically shakes his or her head "no."	**No way, Lady.**
Runs away, leaving the street vacant.	
Discouraged, the ANGELS regroup at the front door of the inn.	

GEORGE

Motions to empty streets.	**Well, that got us nowhere in a hurry.**

ACTIONS	WORDS

PENELOPE

Shivers, then points to the Bethlehem Inn.	**Oh, it's so terribly cold out here. Maybe she went inside that inn to warm up.**

CHANCE

Steps forward.	**I'll go check. You can count on me.**

PENELOPE AND GEORGE

Look at each other, then at Chance.	**Never mind. We'll knock.**
CHANCE shrugs and follows Penelope and George to the front door of the inn. A large "No Vacancy" sign hangs out front.	

INNKEEPER

GEORGE knocks. A crusty old INNKEEPER answers the door.	**Yeah. Wha'dya want?**

GEORGE

	We're looking for a friend of ours.

CHANCE

	She got separated from us in the crowd.

INNKEEPER

Waves hand in disgust. Motions to "building" in town.	**Ah, she ain't in here. I've turned away more people tonight than I can count. Not a room left**

ACTIONS	WORDS

INNKEEPER, continued

Shakes head.	anywhere in this town. Even had to turn away a man with a pregnant woman. She looked ready to deliver any time.

PENELOPE

Stepping forward to challenge the Innkeeper.	You what?! Why, I would have gladly given up my own cloud for a mother-to-be.

INNKEEPER

Steps back, a little frightened by Penelope. Uses thumb to motion back to the Stable scene. Pats self on chest.	Well now, hold your horses there, little Missy. I really felt bad about not having a room for them. So I gave 'em some warm blankets and told 'em they could bed down in my stable for the night. No charge.

PENELOPE

Steps back.	*(Sarcastically)* Oh, I see. Well, in that case, that was kind of you.

GEORGE

	Well, thanks anyway.
The Innkeeper shuts the door.	

ACTIONS	WORDS
Just then the ANGELS hear the introduction music to the song, "We Three Kings of Orient Are."	
The ANGELS stand in awe as THREE KINGS enter from stage right, bearing gifts.	

KING #1	
Motions to audience.	**Please join us in singing, "We Three Kings of Orient Are."**
⑫	**SONG: "We Three Kings of Orient Are"**
When audience sings "following yonder star" the KINGS all point to the star of Bethlehem above the stable.	
On the last chorus the KINGS proceed to stage left and position themselves around the manger. As the song ends, the ANGELS watch with wide eyes as the KINGS go to the Stable scene.	

ALL ANGELS	
⑬ Turn and look at each other, then smack their foreheads with the palms of their hands.	**Of course! The stable!**
The ANGELS hurry to stage left. At the stable, they find Daphne, along with the	

ACTIONS	WORDS
two Shepherds and the Three Kings, honoring the baby lying in the manger in front of MARY and JOSEPH.	
CHANCE	
Pointing to the manger.	**It's a baby!**
DAPHNE	
Turns to audience.	**Please join us in singing, "What Child Is This?"**
	SONG: "What Child Is This?"
GEORGE	
Scratching his head.	**So the birth of this baby is the great event the Archangel was talking about...?**
CHANCE	
Turns to Penelope, questioningly.	**...One of the greatest days in all of creation?**
PENELOPE	
Turns to Chance, scratching her head.	**An event that will save all people on earth?**
DAPHNE	
Gently knocks her head with her fist.	**Knock, knock. Heaven to Angels.**

⑭ appears beside the "SONG" row.
⑮ appears beside the "Scratching his head" row.

ACTIONS	WORDS

ARCHANGEL

Enters stage left, toting four oversized pieces of sheet music.	**This is the Christ. He's the Son of God, sent here to take away the sins of the world. Because of this baby, people will be able to live forever with God. You're witnessing the greatest event of all...God's gift of Love. Mission accomplished, Angels.**
Points to the manger.	
Motions to Angels.	

CHANCE

Holds palms up helplessly.	**Mission accomplished? But I lost the envelope.**

DAPHNE

Excitedly reveals the missing envelope.	**You mean this? I picked it up after it fell out of your pocket. Then I stuffed it in my...**
Starts to realize her blunder	**...pocket and followed...the shepherds...here...oops. Sorry, Chance. I guess I forgot to tell you that I picked up the envelope.**

CHANCE

Pats Daphne on the back.	**It's okay, Daphne. Don't worry about it.**

GEORGE

Shakes Daphne's hand.	**Ditto. In my opinion, it's a fumble-bumble well-done.**

ACTIONS	WORDS
PENELOPE	
Clasps hands and looks at the baby.	**Most definitely. I wouldn't have missed being in this stable tonight for anything—even for the chance to sing in the Heavenly Choir.**
ARCHANGEL	
Claps his hands.	**Bravo! Bravo, my young Angels! You have done well. Your presence here was all that was required. For on this day not only did you share in bearing good tidings, but you witnessed God's greatest gift to all of creation—his Son. Congratulations, my little Angels. You've been promoted. You've each earned a place in the Heavenly Choir.**
The ARCHANGEL hands the Angels their own pieces of sheet music, each personalized with their names on them.	
GEORGE	
Waves music overhead.	**Hallelujah! Sheet Music!**
CHANCE	
Gives George a high-five.	**All right! We're in!**
PENELOPE	
Pulls fist back toward body.	**Yesssss!**

ACTIONS	WORDS

DAPHNE

Calmly looks up.	**Thank you, Lord.**

ALL ANGELS

	Amen.

Four bells chime slowly. The ANGELS excitedly hug each other, joyously hopping and dancing around. The ARCHANGEL smiles proudly.	

CHANCE

A small cry comes from the baby lying in the manger. The ANGELS reverently gather around the baby.	**What's the child's name?**

MARY

Looks up and smiles tenderly at the Angels.	**His name shall be called...Jesus.**

CHANCE

Nods and wipes a tear from his eye.	**This is so cool.**

GEORGE

Puts hand on chest.	**I feel very honored.**

PENELOPE

Kneels to get a closer look at the baby.	**This is a day we will always remember.**

ACTIONS	WORDS

DAPHNE

Claps her hands.	**Baby Jesus. How wonderful.**
FOUR YOUNGER ANGELS excitedly enter from stage right and hurry to the manger.	

YOUNGER ANGELS

	Wow! Look! It's the Christ Child!

YOUNGER ANGEL

Wanders over to the newly promoted Angels and examines their sparkling sheets of music with wonder. Then looks up at the Archangel and tugs on his gown.	**So, when do we get to sing in the choir?**
The ARCHANGEL rolls his eyes.	
CHANCE, GEORGE, DAPHNE, and PENELOPE smile at each other, then each take the hand of a little Angel and join the Archangel front center stage.	

ARCHANGEL

Turns to the audience.	**Please help our choir of Angels rejoice in the newborn King as we sing, "Joy to the World."**
	SONG: "Joy to the World"

Go, Tell It on the Mountain *(by John W. Work, Jr.)*

Chorus:
Go, tell it on the mountain,
Over the hills and everywhere;
Go, tell it on the mountain,
That Jesus Christ is born!

Down in a lowly manger
The humble Christ was born,
And brought us God's salvation
That blessed Christmas morn.

(Repeat Chorus)

While shepherds kept their watching
O'er silent flocks by night,
Behold throughout the heavens
There shone a holy light.

(Repeat Chorus)

Angels We Have Heard on High

Angels we have heard on high,
Sweetly singing o'er the plains,
And the mountains in reply
Echoing their joyous strains.

Chorus:
Gloria in excelsis Deo!
Gloria in excelsis Deo!

Shepherds, why this jubilee?
Why your joyous strains prolong?
What the gladsome tidings be
Which inspire your heav'nly song?

(Repeat Chorus)

O Little Town of Bethlehem *(by Phillips Brooks)*

O little town of Bethlehem,
How still we see thee lie;
Above thy deep and dreamless sleep
The silent stars go by.
Yet in thy dark streets shineth
The everlasting Light;
The hopes and fears of all the years
Are met in thee tonight.

Oh, holy Child of Bethlehem,
Descend to us, we pray;
Cast out our sin, and enter in,
Be born in us today.
We hear the Christmas angels
The great glad tidings tell;
O come to us, abide with us,
Our Lord Emmanuel.

The First Noel

The first Noel, the angels did say,
Was to certain poor shepherds in fields as they lay;
In fields where they lay keeping their sheep,
On a cold winter's night that was so deep.

Noel, Noel, Noel, Noel,
Born is the King of Israel.

We Three Kings *(by John H. Hopkins, Jr.)*

We three Kings of Orient are;
Bearing gifts we traverse afar
Field and fountain, moor and mountain
Following yonder star.

Chorus:
O star of wonder, star of night,
Star with royal beauty bright,
Westward leading, still proceeding,
Guide us to thy perfect light.

Born a King on Bethlehem's plain,
Gold I bring to crown him again,
King forever, ceasing never,
Over us all to reign.

(Repeat Chorus)

Glorious now behold him arise,
King and God and sacrifice,
"Alleluia, Alleluia!"
Earth to the heav'ns replies.

What Child Is This? *(by William C. Dix)*

What Child is this, who laid to rest,
On Mary's lap is sleeping?
Whom angels greet with anthems sweet,
While shepherds watch are keeping?

Chorus:
This, this is Christ the King,
Whom shepherds guard and angels sing.
Haste, haste to bring him laud,
The Babe, the Son of Mary.

So bring him incense, gold and myrrh;
Come, peasant, king, to own him.
The King of kings salvation brings;
Let loving hearts enthrone him.

(Repeat Chorus)

Joy to the World! *(by George F. Handel)*

Joy to the world! The Lord is come;
Let earth receive her King;
Let every heart prepare him room,
And heaven and nature sing,
And heaven and nature sing,
And heaven, and heaven and nature sing.

Joy to the world! the Savior reigns;
Let men their songs employ;
While fields and floods, rocks, hills and plains,
Repeat the sounding joy,
Repeat the sounding joy,
Repeat, repeat the sounding joy.

No more let sin and sorrow grow,
Nor thorns infest the ground;
He comes to make his blessings flow
Far as the curse is found,
Far as the curse is found,
Far as, far as the curse is found.

Permission to photocopy these lyrics from Instant Christmas Pageant: The Fumbly Bumbly Angels granted for local church use. Copyright © Group Publishing, Inc., 1515 Cascade Ave., Loveland, CO 80538.